WOMEN AT WAR
1939–1945

Carol Harris

When the Second World War broke out, in September 1939, women in Britain were expected to play their part by volunteering in a limited range of jobs and duties. They would keep the country going by producing food and weapons, help with air raid precautions, and support military services as auxiliaries. Women would do the jobs of men who could then be sent to fight. They soon proved themselves as capable as men, and the range of jobs they did increased. Women were never to bear arms, but they frequently carried out dangerous work under fire and thousands lost their lives.

In 1941, compulsory National Service was introduced; now the government could send people wherever they were needed. Britain was the only nation to conscript women in this way. They were also expected to run the family home. In wartime this meant queueing for food, and clothing themselves and the family from increasingly scarce resources. In cities and towns especially, it also meant coping with air raids. Anyone with room to spare could be told to provide lodgings for strangers: these might be adults sent to work or to serve in the military, or mothers and children who had been evacuated away from danger areas.

When the war ended people were reunited, often after years of separation. Some had lost everything – family, friends and their homes. Just about all the women of Britain had a job to do and without them, the war could not have been won.

THE THREAT OF WAR

Millions of women volunteered and took paid work to help with the war effort during the First World War of 1914–1918. Then, British women had worked in factories, on the land, running public transport, in offices and supporting the military in non-combatant forces. When the war was over, they also responded, by and large, to the demand that they return to the home.

After the First World War, women were barred from claiming unemployment benefits, and were dismissed from their wartime jobs in many industries, including engineering, printing and munitions. Even in jobs where a woman could traditionally find work, such as teaching or nursing, she had to leave if she married. However, women's contribution in the First World War

greatly bolstered the campaign for Votes for Women. In 1918, women over the age of 30 were allowed to vote. In 1928, the voting age for women was lowered to 21, the same age as men.

Birth control

In the 1920s, newspaper columnists despaired of the morals and preoccupations of young people and in particular, the young women known as 'Flappers' and 'Jazz Babies'. The popular but exaggerated image of the lives of this 'Lost Generation' was of wild parties, sexual promiscuity, drunkenness and drug-taking. Birth control was hotly debated by politicians, feminists, libertarians, the Catholic Church and supporters of the Eugenics movement, such as Marie Stopes. As a result, poorer and working-class married women had access to contraception and advice on family planning for the first time. This enabled them to avoid increasing poverty brought about by a life of serial pregnancy and

▲ Women under the age of 30 voted for the first time in the 1929 'Flapper Election'. The young woman on this contemporary book cover is a typical 'Flapper'.

◄ *This woman operating a milling machine in a Second World War munitions factory had also worked in the First World War, as a capstan lathe operator.*

large families. A woman's place was still 'in the home', looking after her husband and their children. Many women were active in charity work. Organizations such as the Women's Institute were founded at this time.

As the threat of war in Europe increased, the British government called for volunteers to help fight the war and to work in essential industries. Women volunteered in increasing numbers, especially after the 'Munich crisis' of 1938 (see page 4) in which war with Germany was narrowly and temporarily averted. Early in 1939, the government published 'National Service', subtitled 'A guide to the ways in which the people of this country may give service'. For women, it listed Air Raid Precautions (ARP), especially the Women's Voluntary Service, as well as the Auxiliary Fire Service, the Red Cross, the Auxiliary Territorial Service, Royal Air Force companies and the Civil Air Guard; also, the Women's Land Army, service in the Royal Navy

BOVRIL
–"doffs the cap" to the splendid women of Britain

The way in which women are tackling unaccustomed, strenuous and often dangerous war tasks, has merited, and won, widespread admiration. As mechanics, bus conductors, lorry drivers and porters, as W.R.N.S., A.T.S., W.A.A.F., land girls and nurses, and as Civil Defence workers, their record of service is itself an eloquent tribute to the women of Britain. Bovril honours their fine spirit.

▲ *The theme of women on wartime service quickly became popular with advertisers.*

and Auxiliary Hospital Service, and help in evacuating children from dangerous areas. When the Second World War broke out, in September 1939, thousands of women had volunteered but millions would be needed.

3

A CALL TO VOLUNTEER

Planning to defend the British people against aerial attack by bombs or poison gas was at best patchy until 1938, when the new ARP (Air Raid Precautions) Act forced all local councils to draw up detailed schemes for civil defence. At this point, more women than men were volunteering to join such schemes but, overall, the response was poor.

In September 1938, a European war seemed inevitable. However in return for agreement from Britain, France and Italy that he could annexe part of Czechoslovakia, Adolf Hitler promised not to invade anywhere else in Europe. Few believed Hitler, or shared British Prime Minister Neville Chamberlain's view that peace had been secured with this Munich Agreement. War was declared one year later when Germany invaded Poland. In the intervening 12 months, one million people volunteered for ARP duties.

Uniforms in these early days were usually an armband, whistle and tin helmet. Women in ARP were distributing and helping people to fit gas masks, and checking that people observed

▲ *Firefighters at the Holcombe fire station, in Chatham, Kent, practise their drill. The station was run entirely by women.*

the blackout – ensuring no lights were shown so enemy bombers could not easily find their targets. The expected blitzkrieg ('lightning war') and gas attacks did not come with the declaration of war. The months which followed, known as the 'Phoney War', allowed many ARP services invaluable time for recruitment, training and practice.

Keep calm, carry on

When the air raids started, women were out keeping people calm in public shelters, staffing first aid posts and driving ambulances – the vast majority of the Auxiliary Ambulance Service's 10,000 workers were female – while bombs exploded around them and streets blazed.

▲ *Two London Auxiliary Ambulance Service workers tend to a casualty. Rapid treatment, especially to stop blood loss, saved thousands of lives.*

The fire service was severely understrength in the late 1930s. The Auxiliary Fire Service (AFS) was formed to supplement established fire brigades; its women's section, the WAFS, worked from the outset operating switchboards and doing clerical work. Soon women were also running mobile canteens, driving vehicles and operating pumps. Female pump crews were common and in some places stations were run entirely by women. When the National Fire Service was formed in 1941, women had their own ranks and uniforms.

▲ *WVS members prepare hot food in Coventry following air raids, in April 1941. At home and overseas, WVS canteens were seen everywhere throughout the war.*

One of the smaller female civil defence services was the Women's Auxiliary Police Corps. At its height, it had 10,000 members, mainly concentrated in driving and administrative work.

A widely quoted rule was that women volunteers – whether in civilian or military roles – would neither carry nor fire weapons. However, as the threat of invasion grew, this ban was questioned. Edith Summerskill, MP for Fulham West, began the Women's Home Defence League in 1941. The league's main purpose was to assist and support the Home Guard. Its members learned first aid, unarmed combat, Morse code, field cooking and basic weapons skills. They were not given rifles, but were trained to use them.

▲ *Members of the Women's Home Defence League, who were trained in unarmed combat and, controversially, rifle-shooting.*

HOME LIFE

Throughout Britain, people expected that as soon as war was declared, the skies would be filled with enemy planes dropping high-explosive bombs and poisonous gas. So everyone had to have a gas mask and for mothers in particular, this meant persuading reluctant children to carry their masks with them at all times and to put them on if the warning sounded. In the home, windows were taped to stop glass blown out by blast from spreading. If there was room indoors, the Morrison shelter had to be erected, replacing the kitchen or dining room table. Those with a garden might instead have an Anderson shelter, made from sheets of corrugated iron. Many people spent the night in public shelters or left the towns and cities to sleep in hedgerows and fields; during the raids on London, 15,000 people regularly took shelter each night in Chislehurst Caves, in Kent.

Many children were sent away to the countryside. The first such evacuation took place during the Munich crisis in 1938 and was generally

▲ *Children living in cities were sent to live with families in areas away from the bombing. Many were away from their families for years.*

PUTTING OUT FIRES

Incendiary bombs dropped by enemy aircraft would start fires which could easily become major blazes, so in 1941 the government conscripted people into the Fire Guard – teams which watched for, and put out, incendiary bombs quickly. Raids usually took place at night and Rose Uttin, who lived in Wembley, north London, recorded the effects in her diary:

13 August 1944, Up to and including tonight – 56 nights of fire watch for us all in turn ... we fire guards sleep in all our clothes at nights except our shoes and top coats in order to be out of the house in the least possible time – it is two months now since we completely undressed to go to bed ... It is now 11.30 [am] and I am going up to lie on the bed and get a little rest. Talk about turning night into day.

shambolic: afterwards changes were made, such as not letting mothers on to railway platforms to say goodbye to their children. Fears that they might never see each other again prompted tears and many last-minute changes of heart.

On 31 August 1939, with the declaration of war expected at any moment, another more successful evacuation began; millions left the cities and towns, including 12,000 pregnant women and over half a million mothers and children under the age of five.

A long way from home

Wartime brought enormous change to women's traditional role of keeping the home running. Those living in a safe area and with spare rooms would have people sent to live with them: evacuated children, or adults serving in the

▲ A stirrup pump team comprised three people: one to supply the water, one to pump and one to aim the hosepipe.

military, or with civilian jobs that took them a long way from home. Women without children or other relatives to look after were known as 'mobile women'. They might be sent anywhere in the country to work. Those remaining ('immobile women') would soon have work outside the home to do, as well as looking after children and evacuees. The household's meals were planned on a weekly basis and women would spend a long time queuing to buy food. The family sitting at the table

▲ Residents of Hammersmith, London, bring scrap paper and metal for salvage. Tonnes of raw materials were recycled throughout the war.

◄ A family is fitted with gas masks in their Sunderland home. In 1938, masks were distributed to people living in urban areas.

eating together was no longer a daily habit. Many more children began taking school dinners – by early 1945, more than 1.6 million children were eating a meal each day at school.

Separation from family and friends was made harder by the difficulties of keeping in touch. Telephone calls were rarely possible. People kept in contact by letter. Everyone dreaded the official telegram, which might bring news of the death of a loved one.

WOMEN AT WORK

When war broke out in September 1939, the government knew that it was short of the manpower needed to meet the demands of wartime. Women made up 30 per cent of the overall UK workforce before the war but the government hoped initially to fill the gap in essential industries with men who worked in industries where production would decline because of the war. A woman's place was, by common consent, in the home. Just about anywhere they were employed alongside men, women were paid less for doing the same work. In peacetime, some trade union agreements prohibited the employment of women, so in May 1940 a deal was made with the main trade unions to permit employment of women in various kinds of work. But by now it was becoming clear that volunteers could not meet demand and, as volunteers, people might not agree to be sent to places where they were needed.

The newly appointed Prime Minister, Winston Churchill, asked Sir William Beveridge to prepare a secret report on Britain's wartime needs and

▲ *After an air raid, women labourers clean bricks from damaged buildings for recycling. All wear gloves but most do not use their safety goggles.*

the numbers of men available to meet them. He concluded that to meet the increasing demands of civil defence and the armed forces, men would have to be withdrawn from industries such as munitions, which would themselves have to expand. The only solution to meet the shortfall would be to conscript and direct women. Conscription was introduced in 1941. At first, only unmarried women between the ages of 20 and 30 were to be called up. They could choose whether to go into the auxiliary forces or to work in essential industries. In Parliament, the press and elsewhere, the common concern was that conscription of women would lead to the break-up of home and family life. However, by 1943 most of the nation's women were at work.

Caring for children

Crèches and nurseries for the children of working women sprang up in factories or were set up by voluntary organizations and local authorities.

◄ *The drive to increase aircraft production brought thousands of women into the factories.*

EQUAL PAY FOR EQUAL WORK?

By 1943, the range of jobs and numbers of women employed had gone far beyond the scope of the government's original plans. Women were found to be just as productive as the men they had replaced, which prompted calls for them to receive 'equal pay for equal work'. During a parliamentary debate on women in National Service in 1943, Mavis Tate, who chaired the Equal Pay Campaign Committee, said: 'We shall never have real democracy until people are appointed on merit, irrespective of sex.'

The cause was taken up by the more progressive trade unions, some of which changed their rules to allow women to join, and by 1943 nearly two million women were members. Some achieved equal pay with men during the war, including some women bus and tram conductors, women who delivered planes from factories to airfields in the Air Transport Auxiliary and, after 1944, women teachers.

▲ Trousers instead of a skirt are the main feature of the new uniform (shown right) for London's postwomen, which replaced the old uniform (left) in 1941.

▲ A power saw operator cutting steel tubes to make machine tools. The different colours represent different grades of metal.

By 1943, 1,345 nurseries had been established, compared with 14 in 1940. Many women worked part-time or on shifts, as part of flexible working arrangements which were brought in to meet the needs of industry and government. The crucial difference was that, unlike men, women were not routinely deployed away from home to regions in which there was a shortage of labour. Single women ('mobile women') could be directed anywhere; those with children or similar responsibilities were found work nearer to home.

As peace came, the flexible schemes and childcare arrangements were withdrawn and government directed women back to the home. Its priority was to create work for men returning from military service and war work. Some women were able to continue working but most of these did so part-time.

LIVING THROUGH THE BOMBING

▲ *Their premises damaged in air raids, these Norwich shopkeepers traded from old buses.*

Air raids became part of daily life for many years. The towns and cities of Britain, ports and areas where aircraft, tanks and other weapons of war were made were targeted. After the British bombing of Lübeck, a medieval German town of little military value, Britain's historic towns and cities were attacked in revenge. Towards the end of the war, pilotless planes, called V-1s or, more colloquially, 'doodlebugs', were sent over and also, up until the last days of the war, V-2s – rockets which travelled faster than the speed of sound and could devastate streets in one blast.

During the regular bombing raids, people would spend the night in air-raid shelters, or sleeping in fields or cars outside the towns and cities. The WVS (Women's Voluntary Service) branch of ARP took care of people whose homes were badly damaged in air raids ('bombed out'), or who had to leave their homes because an unexploded bomb had landed nearby. Families would go to live with relatives: some would be

temporarily housed in Rest Centres – often in local church or village halls. Originally it was thought that people would stay for just a few days at the centres but many remained for weeks. Those who lost all their clothes would go to clothing stores, where donated clothing would be supplied to them. After air raids, mobile services offering baths, laundry and food would appear.

Fleeing the fires

Electricity, gas and water were often cut off for weeks. Irene Harris had to leave her home near Plymouth in Devon when two oil tanks were bombed, the resulting fires threatening to set light to the village in which she lived: 'We were evacuated into schools where we slept

▲ *Anderson shelters, erected in back gardens, provided a refuge. Alternatively, indoors, a reinforced metal cage called a Morrison shelter often doubled as a dining table.*

▲ *Office workers in Liverpool salvage documents after one of the heavy bombing raids on the port.*

▲ *Dover, in Kent, was frequently bombed and shelled. Seen here are a few of the thousands of people who lived in its chalk caves during the war.*

on the floors. In the morning we would line up for a piece of bread and a slice of corned-beef. We were then taken to Plymouth in coaches to do our work but the factories were all bombed so we lined up at the unemployment offices ...

There was no gas so we lived on stews made on the fire. If we ran out of coal, the meat and vegetables would be put in one dish, your name and address would be written on a piece of paper and stuck on top. This was taken to the local baker, who charged 4 old pence [2p] for cooking it in the bread oven. At 12.30 [pm] the villagers would all gather round the baker and in would go that big shovel that normally brought out the bread ... Oh, the lovely smells ....'

BOMBED OUT

Anne Lee Michell lived in Devon and recorded in her diary going to help a neighbour whose house had been badly damaged in a raid:

21 May 1943, [The house was] ... roofless and windowless and the road littered with debris among which workmen were milling about. I found Peggy, John and Mrs Pope having tea on the lawn at the edge of the tremendous crater with a view of unscathed oaks, woods and hills at their backs! I was hailed with joy by Peggy and after tea helped her pack blankets, move mattresses, china etc in the desolate waste upstairs. Broken glass and plaster everywhere. Great holes in the walls and ceilings. How Mrs P. emerged alive I can't think. Poor old dear, she is very dazed and shocked today but carried on valiantly until the walkers came sightseeing and upset her with tactless remarks about 'your poor old home.' She came up to us in tears and my heart bled for her!

FEEDING THE FAMILY

As soon as war was declared, U-boats – German submarines – began attacking British merchant ships which brought in food from all over the world. The aim was to starve the population into surrender. In November 1939, the British government announced that food rationing would begin in January 1940. This meant that essential food supplies would be fairly distributed and prices controlled. Another important consideration was that people should be fit enough to play their part. For British women, this meant planning the week's food for the family and making sure nothing was wasted. There were classes, leaflets, radio programmes and films showing women how to prepare foods in healthy and appealing ways.

Intermittently, supplies of food were imported from America under the 'Lease-Lend' scheme, or from Canada. Points were allocated for these items – typically, Spam (tinned pork luncheon meat), biscuits or tinned fruit – and shoppers could buy these foods, up to their maximum points allowance.

The 'Dig for Victory' campaign encouraged people to grow their own food, and Women's Institutes ran jam-making sessions when fruit crops were harvested. In millions of homes, lawns and window boxes were turned over to cultivating food. Alternatives to sugar to sweeten cakes and desserts included parsnips (also recommended in recipes for 'mock pineapple') and carrots. Eggless and fatless cakes were made out of necessity and flavourings such as banana essence

would be saved for special occasions. In the countryside, gathering food from hedgerows became popular and recipe books and cookery classes recommended ways of cooking animals and birds not commonly eaten, such as starlings and squirrels.

▲ Collecting ration books from a food office in 1941. The health of the nation improved markedly as a result of government control of food distribution.

How to preserve Tomatoes

MINISTRY OF FOOD · WAR COOKERY LEAFLET 21

When tomatoes are available the wise housewife will preserve some for use in the winter. They are valuable then, not only for the colour and flavour they give to dishes but also for the protective vitamins they contain. Don't forget that you obtain more of the food value from bottled tomatoes if they are eaten "straight from the jar," since further cooking destroys some of their vitamins.

CHOOSING PRESERVING JARS AND RUBBER RINGS

There are many different kinds of preserving jars, but they all work in the same way. The jar, filled with the hot sterilised tomatoes, is closed with a glass or metal lid resting on a rubber ring to make the join airtight; a metal screwband or clip holds the lid tightly in place while the contents of the jar are cooling. When the jar is cold, the lid is held firmly in place by the vacuum formed in the jar; once the jar is sealed in this way it no longer depends on the tightness of the screwband or clip to keep it airtight.

Before buying jars, make sure there are no chips, ridges, etc., on the mouth, which might prevent the lid and rubber ring from fitting properly. If you use the special lids sold to fit on jam jars, choose jars that have smooth and quite circular mouths, and make certain that the lids fit properly.

When buying rubber rings, take a sample jar or ring with you to get the right size. Good rings feel elastic and will spring back after slight stretching.

TESTING JARS BEFORE USE

There is no absolutely reliable way of testing jars before use, but the following may be tried. Fill the jar with water, put on the rubber ring, lid and screwband or

◄ Tomatoes were easy to grow. This Ministry of Food leaflet advises on preserving them in jars in brine and in their own juice.

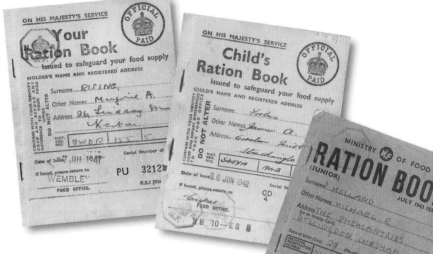

▲ *Left: The standard adult ration book. Pregnant women and nursing mothers, and workers in heavy industry, received extra rations.*

Centre: This ration book is for children from birth to 11 years.

Right: The junior ration book was issued to older children, to be used up to the age of 16.

Healthy eating

From 1942, bread was made with flour containing all the wheatgrain. This was known as the National Loaf and its high wholewheat content was healthier, and required less processing, than the flour for white bread. White bread was now available only for those with special medical needs. The National Loaf was not popular – it did not keep well and was an unattractive grey colour.

Communal feeding caught on: tens of thousands of children now ate midday meals at school; the WVS launched its Meals on Wheels service; factories built canteens – essential to feed those working in shifts round the clock. Cheap, nutritious and unrationed meals were available at British Restaurants. Looked at today, many aspects of the wartime diet are recognizable as essential to healthy eating; it was high in fruit and vegetables, with limited saturated fat and, as war progressed, less and less

sugar. Experts in the emerging science of dietetics advised the government on the importance of a healthy start in life, so pregnant mothers and young children were given extra vitamins in the forms of cod liver oil, orange juice and blackcurrant juice. Child health was monitored through the Boyd Orr study, which found that the children who grew up on the wartime diet were, and remained, healthier than children born before the war.

MAKING DO

Wartime fashion, like wartime food, was about making the best of available resources. It was a fashion based on simple, practical clothing which lasted as long as possible before eventually being imaginatively recycled. In 1940, the government limited the quantities of cotton, rayon and linen that manufacturers could produce for civilian clothing, in 'Limitation of Supply' orders. Prices soared as the shops cleared their stocks and manufacturers concentrated increasingly on their more profitable lines. Clothing was rationed from Whit Sunday, 1 June 1941. To prevent last minute 'panic-buying', there was no advance warning.

Children had their own clothing ration books and expectant mothers were given extra coupons so they could clothe their babies. Clothes or the materials to make them could be bought from any shop but each time the purchaser had to hand over clothing coupons too – the number for each purchase reflecting the amount of work and materials the garment required.

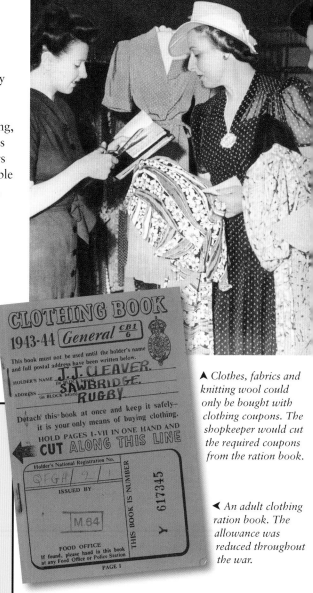

▲ Clothes, fabrics and knitting wool could only be bought with clothing coupons. The shopkeeper would cut the required coupons from the ration book.

◄ An adult clothing ration book. The allowance was reduced throughout the war.

DEFINING FASHION

The Utility scheme was introduced by the Board of Trade. To launch it, the board invited eight leading fashion designers to create garments for a year-round wardrobe for a woman. The results were exhibited and those that were most popular were put into production.

Vogue magazine praised the new simplicity in design and said, 'All women now have an equal chance to buy beautifully designed clothes suitable to their lives and incomes. It is a revolutionary scheme and a heartening thought. It is, in fact an outstanding example of applied democracy.' Throughout the war, Clothing Orders created an increasingly long list of restrictions aimed at producing garments which did not waste material and took as little time as possible to manufacture.

Classes, exhibitions, leaflets and short cinema films appeared on the themes of 'Make Do and Mend' and 'Sew and Save'. The hardships of the inter-war years meant that many poorer women were already well-accustomed to 'making do' but by the end of the war, 50,000 Make Do and Mend classes had been set up, and the Board of

WISE "BUYS"

Coupon-Saving Frocks and Undies

▲ Advice on repairing and reinforcing clothes from Mrs Sew-and-Sew, the iconic character in a host of Board of Trade leaflets.

▲ This 1942 magazine advertisement is for sewing patterns for 'coupon-saving frocks and undies'. Sewing was popular, as fabrics required fewer coupons than ready-made clothes.

◀ The Utility label CC41, known as the Two Cheeses, based on the Civilian Clothing Order of 1941. It appeared on clothes manufactured to government standards.

Trade booklet of that title had sold one and a quarter million copies. Women's magazines were at the forefront of the campaign: in July 1943 the *Home Companion* said, 'Nowadays every re-made garment becomes a uniform of honour and every darn a "decoration",' and the following month it announced that 'patched elbows these days are no disgrace'.

Recycling campaign

Clothing growing children was a particular problem. Before the war, the idea of wearing used clothing was seen as a sign of shameful poverty. In wartime, clothing exchanges run by the Women's Voluntary Services were packed with women trying to find clothes for their children and the search for hand-me-downs and cast-offs dominated everyday conversation.

Knitting was enormously popular, especially of recycled wool. Knitted garments, combining different yarns and colours, became a distinctive wartime fashion.

The government wanted women to cut their hair short but while this was practical when working, women preferred to grow it long and tie it back or put it in a 'snood' (decorative hairnet). That way they could create different styles, especially with a 'perm', a chemical treatment which enabled them to curl, straighten or wave the hair. Hairstyles picked up on current themes throughout the war, from the 'Gas Mask curl', a style which did not interfere with the straps of a gas mask to, later, rolling the hair up in a V ('for Victory') shape. Costume jewellery was another way of decorating a basic simple style, especially fashioned into patriotic designs, such as a plastic V or as an aircraft.

TIME FOR FUN

Cinema, the radio and dancing to live bands or records were by the far the most popular forms of entertainment. Television ceased broadcasting as soon as war was declared. Cinemas and theatres were closed when war broke out because of the potential numbers of casualties which would result if such crowded public places were to be bombed. However, their value in maintaining morale and spreading propaganda meant that they soon opened again. Once a raid started, a message would be put up on the screen so those who wanted to take cover could do so, and the film would continue. Theatre performances would continue in similar fashion.

In 1940, the Council for the Encouragement of Music and the Arts (CEMA) was established to promote British culture. This generally meant more intellectual entertainment and its best-known exponent was the concert pianist Dame Myra Hess. She organized over 1,700 lunchtime classical concerts at the National Gallery in London, herself playing in 150 of them. Her performance at such a concert, attended by the King and Queen, can be seen in the short 1942 film *Listen to Britain*.

Singing and dancing

Pre-war, younger people especially would meet and socialize in dance halls. In wartime, with so many on war work away from home and family, this became an even more popular way of enjoying spare time. For young women especially, entertainment in wartime was remarkably free of restrictions that parents might have insisted on pre-war. Going out to a dance might mean visiting a large purpose-built hall with a sprung floor and an orchestra playing, or, more likely, organizing your own food and drink and bringing some records and a gramophone.

From 1941, the singing star Vera Lynn, already known as the 'Forces Sweetheart', broadcast a radio programme, *Sincerely Yours, Vera Lynn*, in which she sang requests from soldiers, interviewed relatives and read messages to soldiers serving abroad and away from their families. Her popularity with troops was evident on her concert tours overseas throughout the war.

▲ *People often made their own entertainment. Here, women in the London Auxiliary Ambulance Service gather round the piano at their headquarters.*

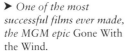

◄ *Robina Hinton (third from right), a professional dancer before the war, with fellow members of ENSA.*

► *One of the most successful films ever made, the MGM epic* Gone With the Wind.

Women went to the cinema more often than men; tickets were cheap, so people would go several times a week to see feature films and newsreels. The government saw this as an opportunity for propaganda, and produced official short films offering advice, such as making the best of rations (Food Flashes) through the Crown Film Unit. Women's new independence was highlighted in films such as *Went the Day Well?*, produced by Ealing Studios, in which the heroic women of the village of Bramley End fought off German invaders and fifth columnists (traitors).

As the war went on, the most popular films were those which offered an escape from the drudgery of daily life. Anna Neagle was already established as a glamorous and sophisticated actress, and she and the comedian George Formby were the most popular British box office stars. American films from Hollywood, with lavish colour and spectacular sets, were extremely popular: the 1939 film *Gone with the Wind*, starring British actress Vivien Leigh, was shown throughout the war.

ENTERTAINING THE TROOPS

The Entertainments National Service Association (ENSA) was set up in 1939 to provide entertainment for British forces. Some of its entertainers, such as Robina Hinton, were already established professionals:

ENSA units could be any size, depending on where they were working. The smallest would travel by lorry, and the lorry would provide the stage; the biggest units travelled by coach and played to the big bases and the garrison theatres, which had excellent facilities ... Costumes just had to be contrived and we used stuff from secondhand shops, cut down and re-used. A new production could apply for an extra allowance of clothing coupons but there was a limit to this.

LENDING A HAND ON THE LAND

The Women's Land Army (WLA) had been created in the First World War and was reformed in 1938. Its aims were to replace farm workers who had been called up for military service, and to help Britain produce more food at home, as imports were threatened by submarine attacks on merchant shipping.

Women were invited to 'lend a hand on the land'. They opted to work in one of several branches of the WLA such as agriculture, producing food for the population, or in forestry. Volunteers were interviewed about their experience and work preferences, locations for work and their uniform size. Some workers lived in private billets, alone or in small groups on farms, smallholdings or in people's homes nearby; some lived in WLA hostels with wardens. They were employed on farms and paid according to nationally set rates.

'We could do with thousands more like you..'

JOIN THE **WOMEN'S LAND ARMY**

▲ A recruitment poster for the WLA. Many WLA members came from towns and cities, and many had only experienced country life on holiday.

WLA wages were not generous: in 1943, women aged 18 or over were guaranteed a minimum weekly wage of 45 shillings (£2.25), which was one third the wage of a man doing skilled work in a factory. From this, deductions were made for board, lodging, laundry and the WLA Benevolent Fund. The official working week was 48 hours in winter and 50 in summer, and Land Girls had holidays and sick pay.

Far from home

Homesickness was a problem. Many volunteers – one-third of whom originally came from cities and towns – had never been away from home before.

▲ WLA member Rose Markovitch operating a cub excavator. The government took control of farming in the Second World War in order to modernize food production.

▲ *Entire farms were worked by 'Land Girls'. These women are haymaking and one of them is driving the tractor.*

▲ *This plastic badge was awarded to WLA members who completed specialist training.*

Many discovered that working in the countryside was very different from visiting it on holiday. The WLA produced a magazine, *The Land Girl*, which was popular. Locally, supervisors would visit the volunteers and their employers regularly to discuss problems. The life meant long days of hard physical work but many former Land Girls say that as they became fitter, they enjoyed the experience, and they ate better than their families at home.

In the early days, the system was not well organized. Many WLA volunteers completed four to six weeks of training and then waited to be sent to work. Others were allocated to farms where they were not yet needed, and were not welcomed by farmers and the workers they were sent to replace. As the war progressed, the government mechanized farming and organized it on a national scale, to maximize food production. WLA training courses involved practical and oral examinations in every aspect of farming, from rearing cattle, thatching and pest control, to cultivating fruit and bee-keeping. The WLA was soon essential in keeping farms running and producing food and much of the major shift to home production of the nation's food was down to their efforts. Even so, food shortages continued and actually worsened after the war, so the Women's Land Army was not disbanded until 1950.

THE WOMEN'S TIMBER CORPS

The Women's Timber Corps branch of the WLA, whose members were often known as 'Lumber Jills', was formed in 1942. It produced timber for use as pit props, ships' masts, railway sleepers and telegraph poles. Many members were based in Scotland and lived in wooden huts, in camps in remote areas .

Their training involved learning to use traditional, mainly manual, tools. The WTC's work involved felling trees, stripping the branches, loading lorries and sawmilling timber. Some were specialists, trained to measure the amount of timber in a tree and the amount of timber felled, and to survey new woodlands and select trees for felling. Their expertise was in demand abroad as well as at home and some were sent overseas to help with post-war reconstruction, until the WTC wound up in 1946.

▲ *Despite mechanization, much of the work of the Timber Corps was hard manual labour.*

KEEPING THINGS MOVING

Trains and buses were usually packed with passengers in wartime and services were frequently disrupted. People were told to avoid making unnecessary journeys, but even so, public transport was an essential part of daily life. Few people had cars and petrol was strictly rationed. Tens of thousands of women were sent to work on the railways and buses. They were not allowed to drive them but did just about every other job. The vast majority of bus conductors, known as 'clippies', were female. Women also worked in engineering, maintaining and repairing damaged vehicles at bus depots and goods yards, and in the transport companies' own factories.

At the end of the war, one of the country's main railway companies, the LMS (London, Midland and Scottish), recorded that with so little time for training, women were at first directed into simpler jobs, however: 'They finally worked in nearly 250 different railway grades, including such diverse jobs as concrete workers, sailmakers

▲ *In the UK and overseas, Air Transport Auxiliary pilots flew planes of all sizes between air bases, and factories where aircraft were manufactured and repaired.*

THE AIR TRANSPORT AUXILIARY

Female pilots such as Amy Johnson, the first woman to fly solo from England to Australia, had become famous in the 1930s for their exploits, tackling long, arduous journeys. They inspired women who could afford the lessons to get a pilot's licence.

The Air Transport Auxiliary was formed in 1939 and at first comprised male civilian pilots whose job was to ferry people and messages in light aircraft around the country. Soon, the ATA was doing essential work flying planes from the factories producing them to military airfields, and initial reluctance to allow women to play their part was overcome. Anyone with a pilot's licence and over 200 hours flying time could apply, and by 1944, 108 of the ATA's 609 pilots were women. By the end of the war, ATA pilots had flown 309,011 aircraft. Many had died on duty, including Amy Johnson, reported missing in 1941.

(the rail company also had its own fleet of ships), assistant architects, fitters, electricians, boiler cleaners, weighbridge men, painters, lock-keepers, stablemen and even blacksmiths. At one time the total number employed by the company amounted to 39,000, some 17 per cent of the whole staff.'

Rivers and canals had been used less and less before the war but wartime meant they were needed once more to move supplies across the country. Women took on the job of bargees. Cargo totalling more than 12 million tonnes was carried every year on the waterways of Britain. The work was dirty and exhausting – over half the cargo transported in this way was coal and coke.

▲ Women bargees earned a basic wage of £3 a week. They lived and worked on canal narrowboats in crews of three.

▲ Most bus conductors were women. They were known as 'clippies' because they clipped passengers' tickets to show where they had boarded.

Deaths at sea

Women had worked in the Merchant Navy before the war and were among the first casualties. Just a few hours after the declaration of war the liner *Athenia* was torpedoed and sunk by a German U-boat in the Atlantic Ocean and four women –

stewardesses Alison Harrower, Margaret Johnston, Jessie Lawler and Hannah Baird – died. Merchant Navy shipping was constantly under threat of attack and so travelled in convoys which could be given some protection by Royal Navy vessels. Even so, a merchant ship in the North Atlantic was one of the most dangerous places to be.

At first, evacuation of children across the sea to the USA and Canada by ship was organized by the Children's Overseas Reception Board. Then, in September 1940, the passenger liner *City of Benares* was sunk by a U-boat and 258 died, including 77 of the 90 evacuees on board, and the film director Ruby Grierson, who was making a film about the evacuees' journey. As a result of the sinking, overseas evacuation of children ended.

◀ Railway porters working for the London, Midland and Scottish railway. Although women did most jobs, they were not allowed to drive the trains.

WOMEN IN KHAKI

The Auxiliary Territorial Service was created in 1938 with the aim of releasing men in the services from 'routine duties' – mainly cooking, clerical, storekeeping and laundry work – so they could be sent to fight. ATS volunteers were paid one third less than men in the army in similar ranks and received 20 per cent less food rations. The government hoped for 25,000 volunteers but in this early stage only 17,000 came forward. Even so, after completing the required forms, passing the interview and medical, and receiving training, many women were sent home again as the services did not have enough uniforms. They were given a list of their own clothes to bring when reporting for duty if war broke out before they had been issued with them.

When war was declared, a few ATS recruits were soon sent into action: some went over to France with the British Expeditionary Force and others were sent to North Africa. But by the end of 1940, well over a quarter of volunteers had left because of continuing problems in

▲ Abram Games' famous recruitment poster presented a glamorous image of the ATS.

supplying uniforms, poor accommodation and homesickness. However, their contribution was beginning to be valued and the number of roles was expanding. In 1941, defence regulations were amended to give the ATS military status and the service was revamped under a new director, Jean Knox. She improved conditions, including accommodation and supplies of uniform, and gave the service a smart new image. Women from abroad were allowed to join, too, including 1,000 who were refugees from Nazi Germany.

Searchlight duty

The ATS was deployed in anti-aircraft batteries – where the women worked on every aspect except actually firing the guns – and in searchlight batteries.

▲ A major part of the ATS served in anti-aircraft batteries such as this one. ATS women did every job in the battery.

▲ *ATS officers spent six weeks of their training on a search light site, learning the jobs of those they would command.*

They particularly welcomed the introduction of the 'teddy-bear' coat to the ATS uniform. This was a fake fur woollen overcoat, issued to the ATS who had been on duty in all weathers wearing only, at best, their official raincoats.

Many ATS worked alongside male soldiers but the 93rd Searchlight Regiment consisted entirely of women. They sent massive beams into the sky to pick out enemy aircraft or guide friendly planes safely home. The job involved operating the searchlight manually, running the generator that powered it, throwing the switch that sent the

DANGEROUS AND SECRET WORK

The First Aid Nursing Yeomanry operated alongside the ATS throughout the war. The FANY was a much older organization, founded in 1907. The plan at the beginning of the Second World War was for the Motor Driver Companies of the ATS to be formed from the FANY and these eventually became the Mechanized Transport Corps. But others, known as the Free FANY, remained independent of the ATS. From this group came many of the women who undertook dangerous and secret work in the Special Operations Executive (SOE). They worked in enemy territory as saboteurs and radio operators, conducting agents and linking with local resistance groups. Twelve members of FANY died in Nazi concentration camps. Three FANY were awarded the George Cross, two of them posthumously.

▲ *The shoulder flash worn by members of the First Aid Nursing Yeomanry.*

beam upwards, tracking aircraft on radar, and maintaining the equipment.

By the end of 1943, the ATS had over 200,000 auxiliaries and 6,000 officers, covering more than 80 trades. Some ATS joined the British contingent working with American forces under the command of General Eisenhower in the Supreme Headquarters Allied Expeditionary Force (SHAEF). Among them was Mary Bateman, whose aptitude for taking down coded messages accurately and quickly was invaluable. This posting had advantages: 'We had PX [US Forces] rations the same as their troops ... we had about seven chocolate bars a week and as sweets etc were rationed [at home], we felt we had died and gone to heaven!'

◄ *ATS women looking out for enemy aircraft. Unusually, the women have no insignia on their uniforms.*

BOMBS AND BALLOONS

The Women's Auxiliary Air Force (WAAF) was formed in June 1939. Women initially were needed for driving, clerical and domestic work. The following year, the Battle of Britain, in which the German airforce attempted to gain control of the airspace over Britain, led to a rapid expansion of roles for WAAFs. Many were drafted into the newly formed Royal Observer Corps, which replaced the volunteer Observer Corps. Soon WAAFs were launching and flying barrage balloons. These were huge, hydrogen-filled structures on steel hawsers which formed barriers to aircraft. Enemy bombers had to fly above them, which took the aircraft up within range of anti-aircraft guns. WAAF mechanics became a familiar sight, maintaining and repairing aircraft. WAAFs were also put to work interpreting reconnaissance photos and packing parachutes, and WAAF officers would debrief returning air crews.

WAAFs listening on headphones and plotting the course of an aerial battle on a vast table-top map is a familiar image from the Second World War. The work could be harrowing: listening to the radio transmissions of aircrew – friendly and enemy – as they were shot down, or tracking a pilot who did not know that he was flying into an area where the enemy waited to pounce, was an everyday experience for some.

Jobs galore

Recruitment advertising emphasized training for a worthwhile job: 'It doesn't matter what your job was in civil life. There are 48 different jobs in the WAAF including radio operators, plotters, drivers, clerks, cooks and orderlies. Don't hang

◄ *A WAAF engineer changes the spark plugs on a training aircraft. Before the war, this woman was an office worker.*

◄ *A WAAF telegraph operator. Telegraphists took down and transmitted coded messages. They wore a flash on their sleeve, below the albatross of the RAF.*

▼ *In the mapping room, a WAAF plots the messages she receives over her headset.*

MILITARY MEDALS FOR SOME

Extract from a talk by a flight officer in the WAAF, broadcast on the BBC in November 1940:

Plotters particularly have proved that those members of the RAF were justified who said that women could be trusted to carry out operational work in air raids. They have shown they have plenty of nerve. So, too, have the telephone operators. Those WAAF who got the Military Medal this week were all telephone operators and it is a good thing they kept their heads and stuck to their job because the station defence really depends on them. As for the plotters, I know one who had half a table where she was working bombed away, but she went on with her job. Two others had a shed blown down over them but when they were dug out they were still sticking to what they had been doing before the bomb fell.

King's Regulations and the manual of Air Force Law. There were examinations in all subjects, endless drill inspection and physical training. By the time we were commissioned we were expected to take a parade and to know all the basic drill movements.'

As the war took the RAF overseas, the WAAF went with them. Some took on the highly dangerous work of serving with the Special Operations Executive (SOE) and won medals from the French and the British governments.

back because you feel the WAAF only wants experts. It can soon make an expert out of you.' Like the ATS, the WAAF underwent a massive expansion in numbers and trades, reaching a peak of 180,000 in 1943. Hoping to become an officer, WAAF Betty Sharp was sent to the Officer Cadet Training Unit at Grange-over-Sands: 'Everything was completely different: the style of living was designed to get us used to life in an officers' mess and we appreciated the comparative comfort. The course lasted four weeks. The lectures covered all aspects of service life and the responsibilities of an officer. We spent a lot of time studying

▲ *At first WAAFs made and repaired barrage balloons but they were soon also trained to fly them.*

WRENS ON LAND AND SEA

The Women's Royal Naval Service (WRNS), whose members were known as Wrens, was by far the smallest of the three women's services. It had been the first of the armed forces to recruit women in the First World War, initially for duties on shore. It was reformed in 1939, when it appealed for women volunteers under the slogan 'Free a Man for the Fleet'. Three thousand women were quickly recruited, including some who, having served in WWI, enlisted with their daughters. They were expected to be cooks and stewards, despatch riders, sailmakers, and in intelligence. They were also recruited to new roles such as radio operators, meteorologists, bomb range markers, sea-going cipher officers, and coders. Many were Boat's Crew Wrens, working in smaller craft taking people and supplies between large ships and the shore.

▲ *Wrens paint a landing craft during 18 weeks of training as 'ship mechanics', in which they also learned about welding, sign writing and wood-machining.*

◄ *As in other women's wartime services, Wrens were recruited so that men could to be sent on active service.*

Recruits were given a medical examination and two weeks' training, including squad drill, PT (physical training) and lectures about the Royal Navy. Vera Laughton-Mathews, its director, had served in the First World War as a Wren. She was, by now, the head of the Girl Guides Association and had been an active suffragette. She battled with the Admiralty, resisting moves to designate Wrens as volunteers and civilians, and campaigned successfully for WRNS officer training to be set up at the Greenwich naval school, and for married women with children, of whom she was an example, to be allowed to join.

WOMEN'S · ROYAL · NAVAL · SERVICE

join the Wrens

AND · FREE · A · MAN · FOR · THE · FLEET

APPLY TO DIRECTOR W.R.N.S. ADMIRALTY S.W.I.
OR THE NEAREST EMPLOYMENT EXCHANGE

▲ *In hot climates, women in the auxiliary forces wore 'tropical kit' – seen here in the white dresses of these Wrens, off duty in Sri Lanka.*

another family member in the Royal Navy or Merchant Navy, past employment as a cook or in domestic service, or qualifications in the German language. However, the demand for Wrens was such that by mid-1942 there was a shortage. The WRNS continued to expand and, in 1944, had 74,000 members.

One of the most important roles was at Bletchley Park – the Government Code and Cipher School in Buckinghamshire. Here, Wrens worked as part of ULTRA, the name given to the high-level intelligence produced at Bletchley. They intercepted and took down coded messages for decryption and so played a vital role in breaking the 'Enigma' cipher, the means by which the German military communicated. As with the other services, much of the work was tedious and physically hard but the WRNS retained its glamorous image throughout. By the end of the war a total of 100,000 women had served in the WRNS, in any one of nearly 200 different jobs, many of them overseas.

Call for Wrens

When conscription was introduced in 1941, the WRNS had a waiting list of applicants, unlike the ATS and WAAF. Those wanting to join had to have either past service in the WRNS or Admiralty, practical experience of boat work,

▶ *The distinctive tricorn hat worn by WRNS officers was chosen for the service by Queen Elizabeth, mother of Queen Elizabeth II.*

WRENS ON THE ROAD

In 1945, Gwyneth Verdon-Roe, her wartime service as a WRNS plotter ended, trained as a WRNS driver and mechanic. She wrote to her mother:

Our bus driver instructor, Len, is the nicest, kindest, most patient man imaginable. He says girls learn to drive more quickly than the men he has taught. I felt as proud as Punch sitting in this enormous great lorry, Len sitting beside me looking nervous ... Today I drove 20 miles [32km] through traffic, and lights, and awkward turnings, with convoys on the road, through Hendon, Finchley and Wembley. The afternoon was spent in the classroom learning about Safety First and tomorrow we start on the mechanical dirty work, lying on our backs under the car getting gloriously oily.

CASUALTIES OF WAR

War creates an inevitable increase in demand for nurses, military and civilian, and the profession's leaders took the opportunities provided by the Second World War to push for major improvements in nurses' training, pay and conditions. So severe was the shortage of nurses in 1939 that a government inquiry recommended sweeping reforms to attract more women to the profession, including national pay scales, leave entitlement and shorter hours. It also recommended changes to training and called for an end to petty and often meaningless restrictions. The Civil Nursing Reserve was created to provide nursing assistants, mainly for civilian hospitals and Air Raid Precautions first-aid posts. Nursing detachments of the British Red Cross Society and St John Ambulance Brigade helped to fill the gaps.

▲ *Nurses clear their bombed hospital after an air raid. Patients were evacuated from danger areas but hospitals still received casualties.*

Military nurses served in the UK and abroad, in British military hospitals, on hospital ships and in field hospitals. Each branch had its own nurses: the army had the QAIMNS (Queen Alexandra's Imperial Military Nursing Service); the navy, QARNNS (Queen Alexandra's Royal Naval Nursing Service); and the RAF had the PMRAFNS (Princess Mary's Royal Air Force Nursing Service).

Adrift at sea

Postings overseas could be an opportunity to work in a big military hospital and enjoy the sights and social life of the city in relative safety. But the journey was perilous, as this 1944 account, written by a nursing sister in the QAIMNS, shows. Her ship was torpedoed and she spent 12 days in a lifeboat with 53 men and minimal medical supplies before they were rescued. She wrote: 'I held sick parade and any men "off colour" did not row that day and had double water rations ... The men came out in boils and it was agony for them to sit and row.

◄ *These WAAF nurse orderlies are taking an RAF casualty to a hospital. WAAF nurse orderlies were specially trained in air ambulance work.*

► *Royal Army Medical Corps nurses irrigate a soldier's eye.*

I put a safety pin in iodine and got the core out, every two hours soaked the place in salt water and in two days it healed. The sunburn on their chests became septic; there was one little tube of Tananfax and I put a smear on and the next day treated it two-hourly with salt water.'

Military nurses achieved better pay and status during the war but attempts to reform civilian nursing had less impact. The vast majority of doctors were male but, once again, necessity in wartime meant women doctors filled more senior positions than would otherwise have been open to them, and proved they could do the job. Even so, in April 1943 the British Medical Journal reported that Frederick Bellenger MP 'had condemned the medical examination of men in the army by women Medical Officers'. For the government, the Secretary of State for War Arthur Henderson replied that, in future, serving men and women would have the right to be examined by medical officers of their own sex.

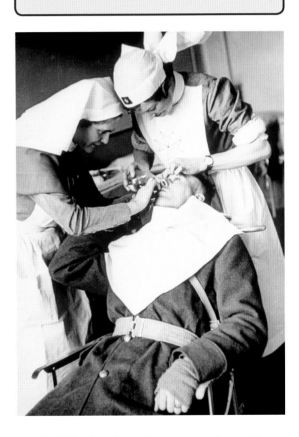

In 1944, the Goodenough report on the training of doctors said that government funding should only be given to medical schools which admitted 'a fair proportion' of women students, and all hospital posts for qualified doctors should be open equally to men and women.

LOVE AND MARRIAGE

War, separation and the knowledge that one might not live much longer influenced people's attitudes to love and sex. Younger women, especially, could enjoy more unchaperoned freedom to form attachments than they would otherwise have experienced. There were many opportunities to meet and socialize. Dances at a local hall or military base could bring hundreds of people together. Men and women were sent to live away from home on military or civilian wartime service, which greatly increased the populations of small towns and villages. Romances were punctuated by the boredom of being separated and the knowledge that death might prevent a reunion. Some relationships were brief and light-hearted; some endured, despite separation and only occasional communication by letter.

Wartime weddings were modest events with a few guests – many friends and relatives would be away or working, unable to attend because of

▲ *This wartime bride, Miss Freda Day, and groom, ARP stretcher-bearer Mr E. G. Hall, are carried by fellow stretcher-bearers on their wedding day.*

the difficulties of travelling, or unwilling to do so because of the threat of bombing.

Shortages meant that weddings had to be carefully planned, even though a few extra rations might be allocated for the occasion. Friends and relatives contributed, saving special treats such as dried fruit and alcohol. Bakers would hire out a cardboard box decorated like a traditional tiered 'wedding cake' with a real, smaller plain fruitcake concealed in the bottom tier.

'OVERSEXED AND OVER HERE'

Allied troops from other nations were a regular sight in Britain during the war. American soldiers were known as GIs and were often popular. They were smartly dressed and knew the latest dances. An American soldier would have cigarettes, chewing gum, stockings and chocolate as gifts for the local population. Permanent relationships were discouraged but, even so, some endured and at the end of the war an estimated 70,000 British women who married GIs went to join their husbands in a new life in the USA.

▲ *Polish airmen and local women meet on the staircase at the famous Tower Ballroom in Blackpool, in 1943.*

"I'm sure I'm losing him : last night he only said Good night twice."

"That's him, 'Hamm and Eggs Smith, V.C.' but he's too scared to tell Dad!" We're engaged.

▲ *Brief but intense relationships between people who had only just met were the norm in wartime. Not all the conventions of young love and marriage were swept away. These illustrations are cartoons taken from wartime magazines.*

Flowers and other decorations would be collected and made, often by gathering from domestic gardens, as commercial flower growers had turned just about all their land over to food production. Traditional wedding dresses needed too much material to be made specially. Many brides hired dresses; a few married in dresses made from salvaged parachutes. A smart two-piece suit decorated with a suitable corsage doubled as a wedding dress and going-away outfit. Often bride and groom were in uniform and guests, too, might be in their work dress as the smartest clothes they had. Once married, a couple often had little time to spend together on honeymoon before they went back to their respective wartime occupations.

... and divorce

As the war ended, divorce rates went up sharply. The armed forces introduced a form of 'quickie divorce' for couples who, by mutual agreement, wanted to end their marriage. Sexual behaviour was also changed by wartime circumstances. Sexual health became a major concern as rates for sexually transmitted diseases went up. Sex education was made more explicit, leaving many people much better informed than they might otherwise have been.

There was a stigma attached to an unmarried woman having a baby, so weddings might take place because of an unplanned pregnancy. Even so, the number of unmarried women giving birth soared. Doctors would prescribe female contraception to married women only. Condoms were issued to serving men, but rubber shortages meant that male contraceptives, too, were not freely available to all. Abortion was illegal in most circumstances. Typically for wartime, prostitution increased, encouraged by the presence of millions of unattached servicemen with free time and money to spend.

PEACE AND RECONSTRUCTION

The end of the war meant an end to a way of life. Some women continued working but most had to give up their jobs. Many women had travelled abroad or found that the mixing of social classes at home had broadened their horizons and changed attitudes. Rebuilding family life was sometimes difficult. Married women were reunited with husbands and evacuated children returned home, often after years of separation. People wanted to get on with their own lives. Between 1946 and 1950, there was a huge rise in births in Britain, described as the post-war baby boom.

In 1945, a Labour government, committed to introducing the NHS (National Health Service) and modernizing the welfare state, was voted in. Expectations were high but the country was bankrupt. Shortages worsened and rationing increased as Britain struggled to reconstruct industries and generate income through exports.

Permanent women's military services were established. In 1949, the WRNS was reformed, the Auxiliary Territorial Service was replaced by the Women's Royal Army Corps, and the WAAF was replaced with the Women's Royal Air Force. Some wartime services, such as the ARP-based Women's Voluntary Service, continued in Britain and abroad. Later, women's experiences of working in wartime contributed to the debate which, in the 1970s, led to legislation introducing equal pay and outlawing sex discrimination.

Back Cover: A woman paints a roundel on a Spitfire aeroplane.

▲ *Adults and children alike took part in street parties celebrating victory in Europe and then victory over Japan a few months later in 1945.*

Acknowledgements

Written by Carol Harris. The author has asserted her moral rights.
Edited by Shelley Grimwood.
Designed by Jemma Cox.
Picture reseach by Carol Harris and Shelley Grimwood.

Photographs reproduced by kind permission of Carol Harris except for: Alamy, FC (Pictorial Press); Crown copyright, 3, 6, 12c, 15t, 18tr, 22tr, 23t, 26b; Getty Images, IFC (Planet News), 5 both (Popperfoto), 7bl (SSPL) & cr, 12/13tc, 16bl, 17tr, 19br, 21tr, 23bl, 29br, 30b (Popperfoto); Kent Messenger, 4t.

Every effort has been made to contact the copyright holders; the publisher will be pleased to rectify any omissions in future editions.

Text © Pitkin Publishing.

Publication in this form © Pitkin Publishing 2013.

Printed in China.

ISBN: 978-1-84165-379-2   1/13